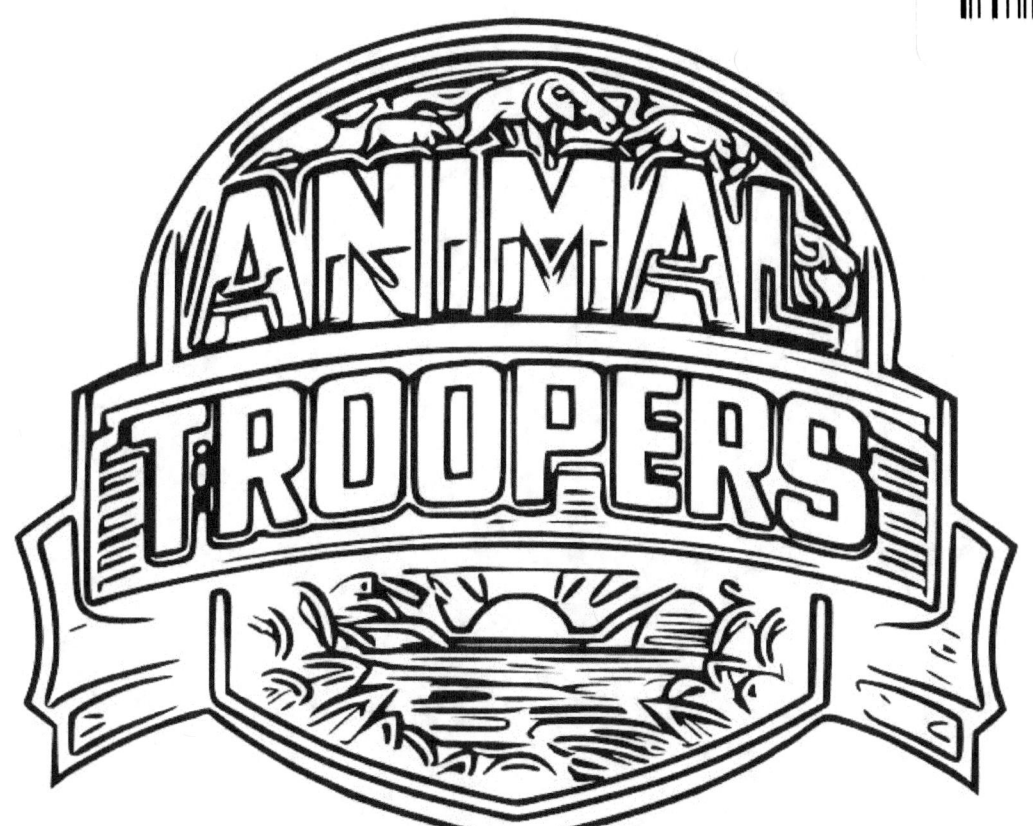

MEET THE PLATOON

RED   MAC   LEO
BLITZ   HOPPER   ROAR
TUBS   RAMPAGE   SOAR
KONGA   BOBO   FUZZY
CHARGE   SNAPPER   CRUNCH
SHADOW   OINK   CHICKADEE
ROUGHSKIN   SHELLSHOCK

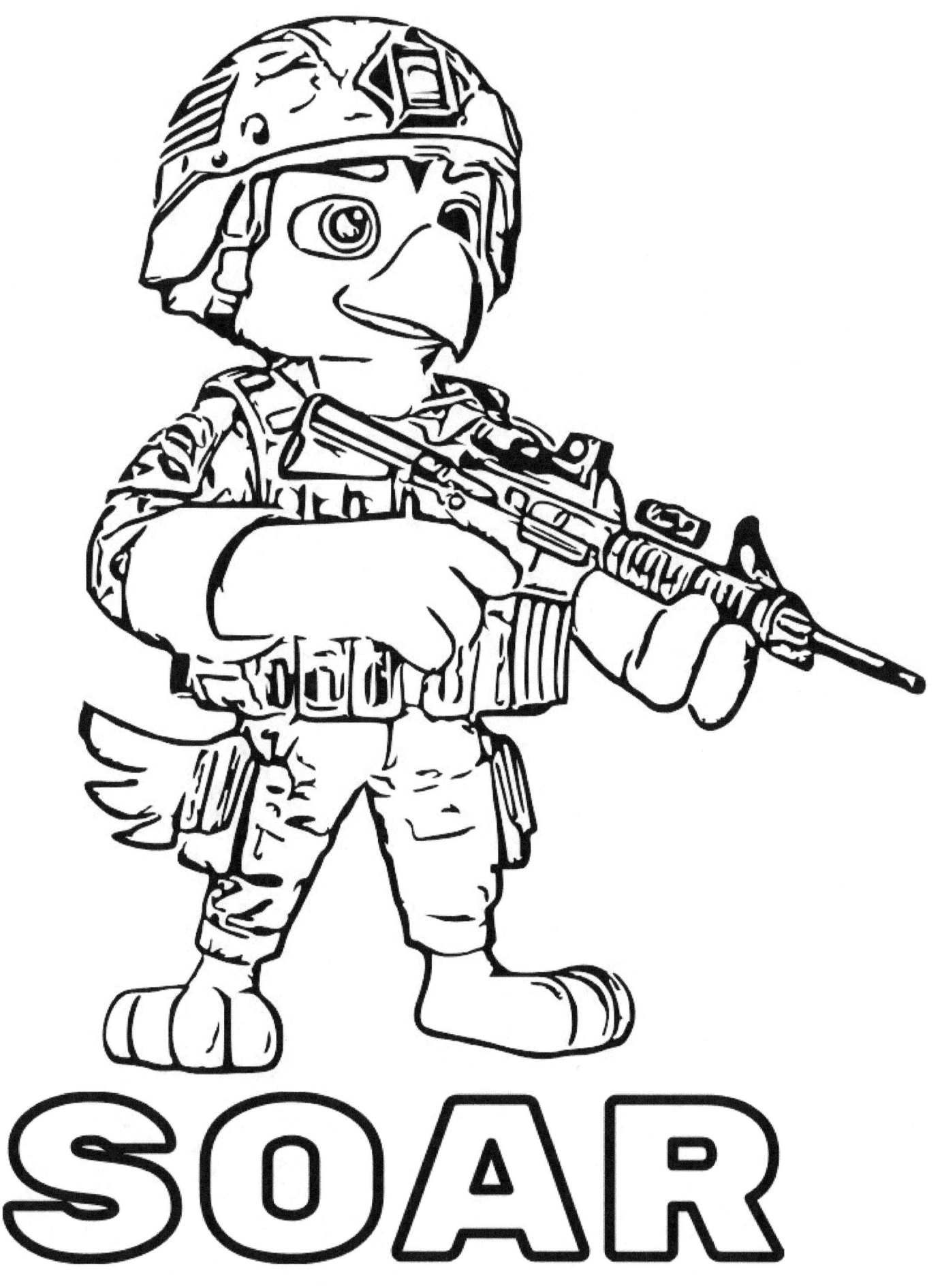

SOAR

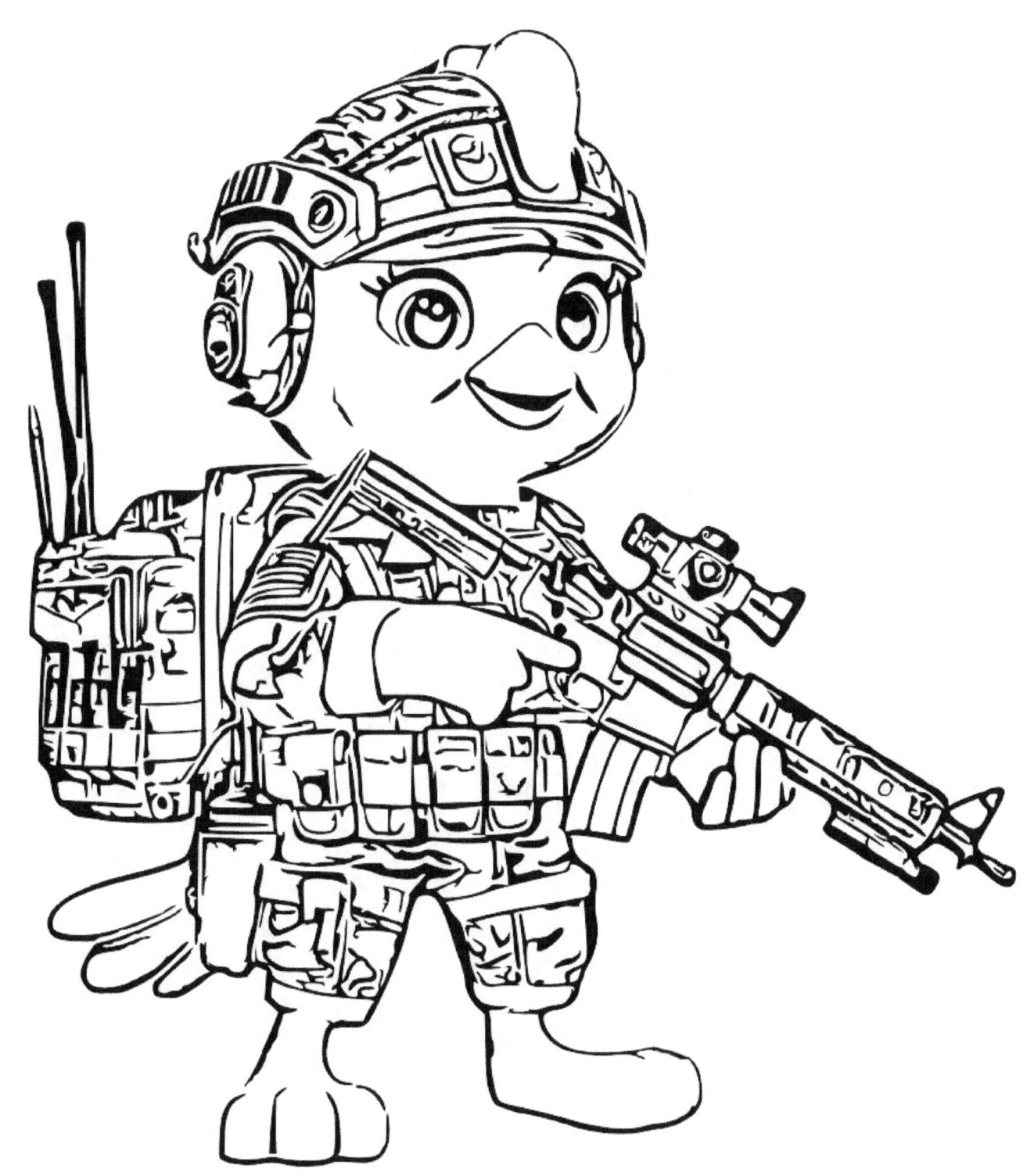

CHICKADEE

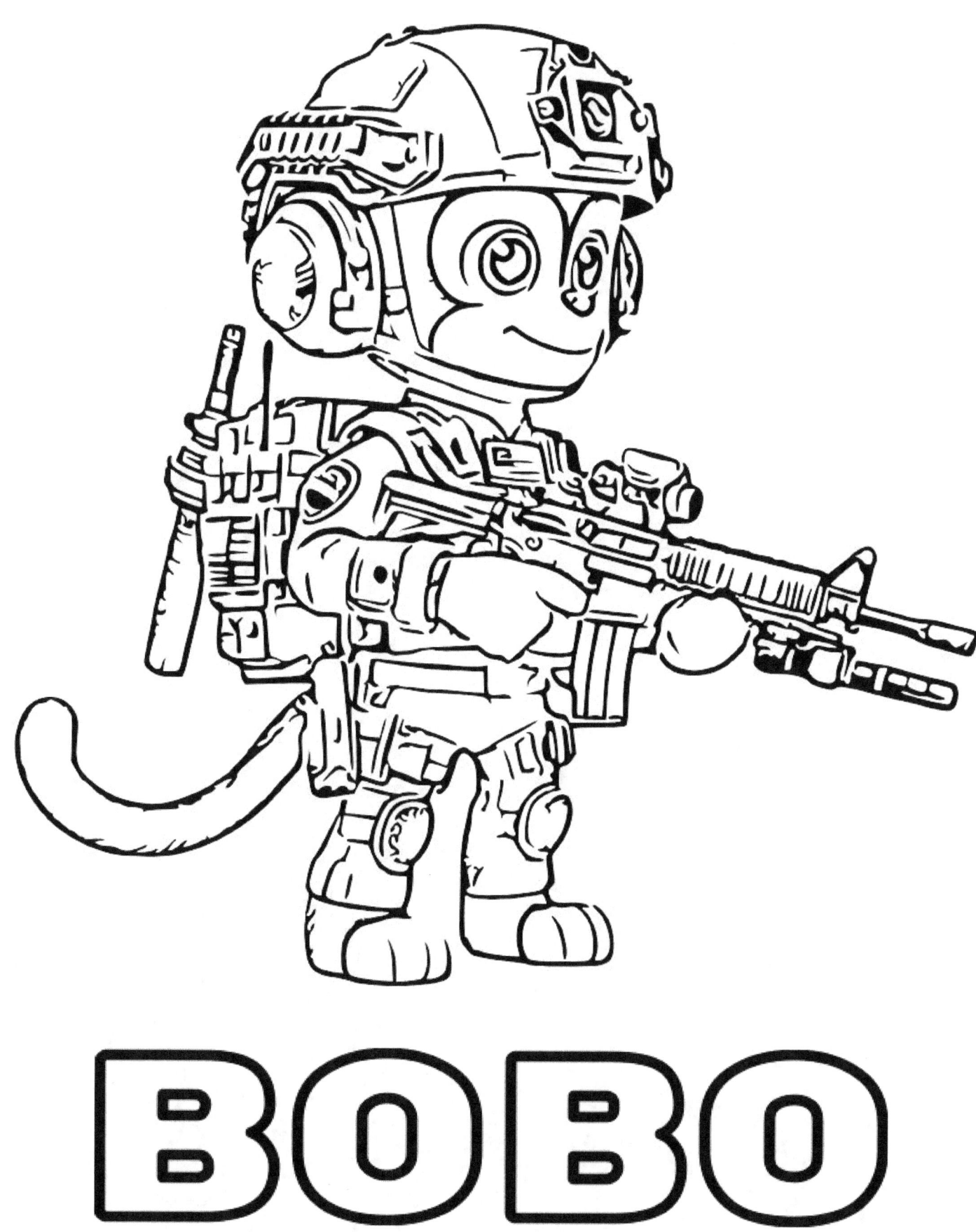

BOBO

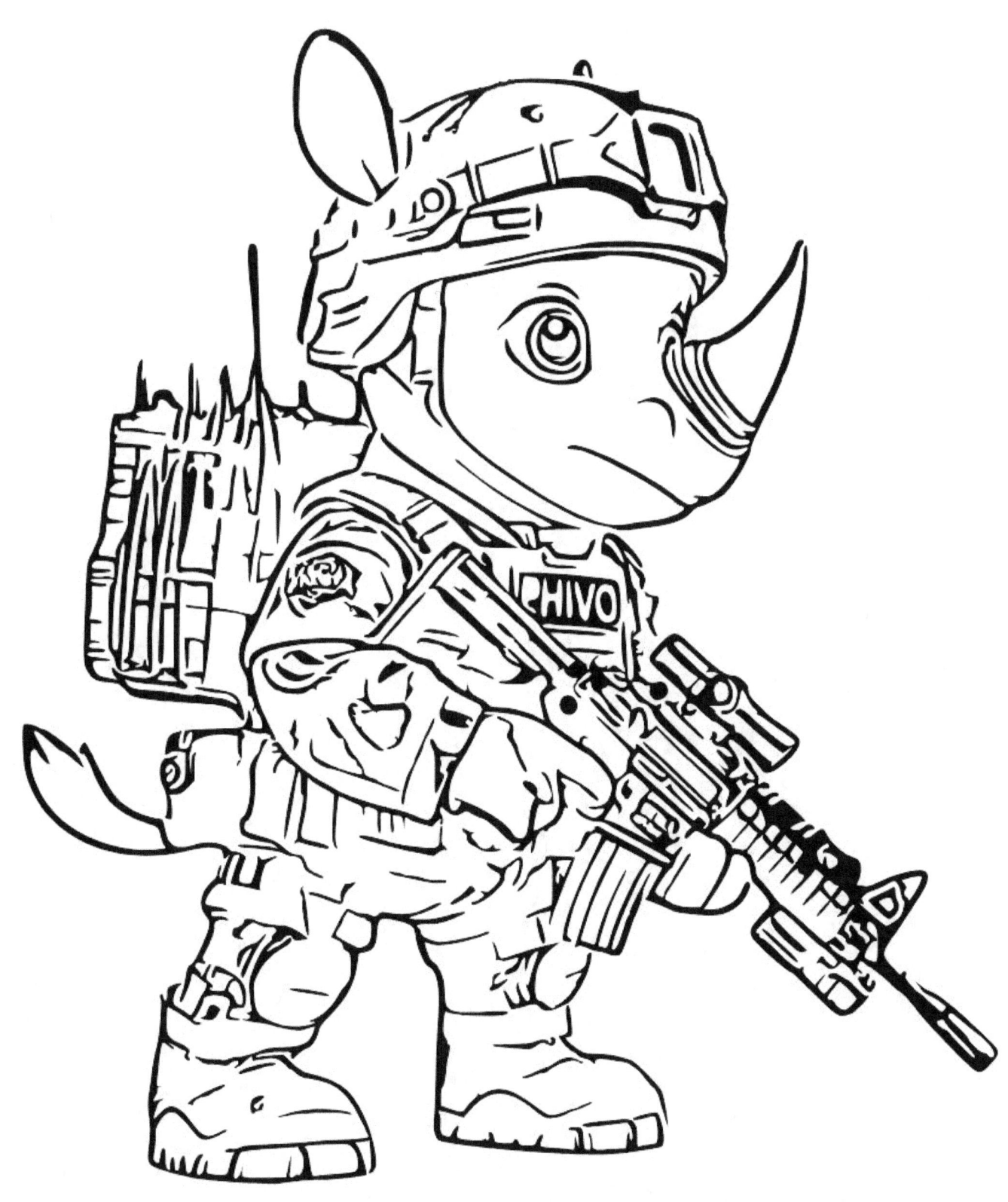

CHARGE

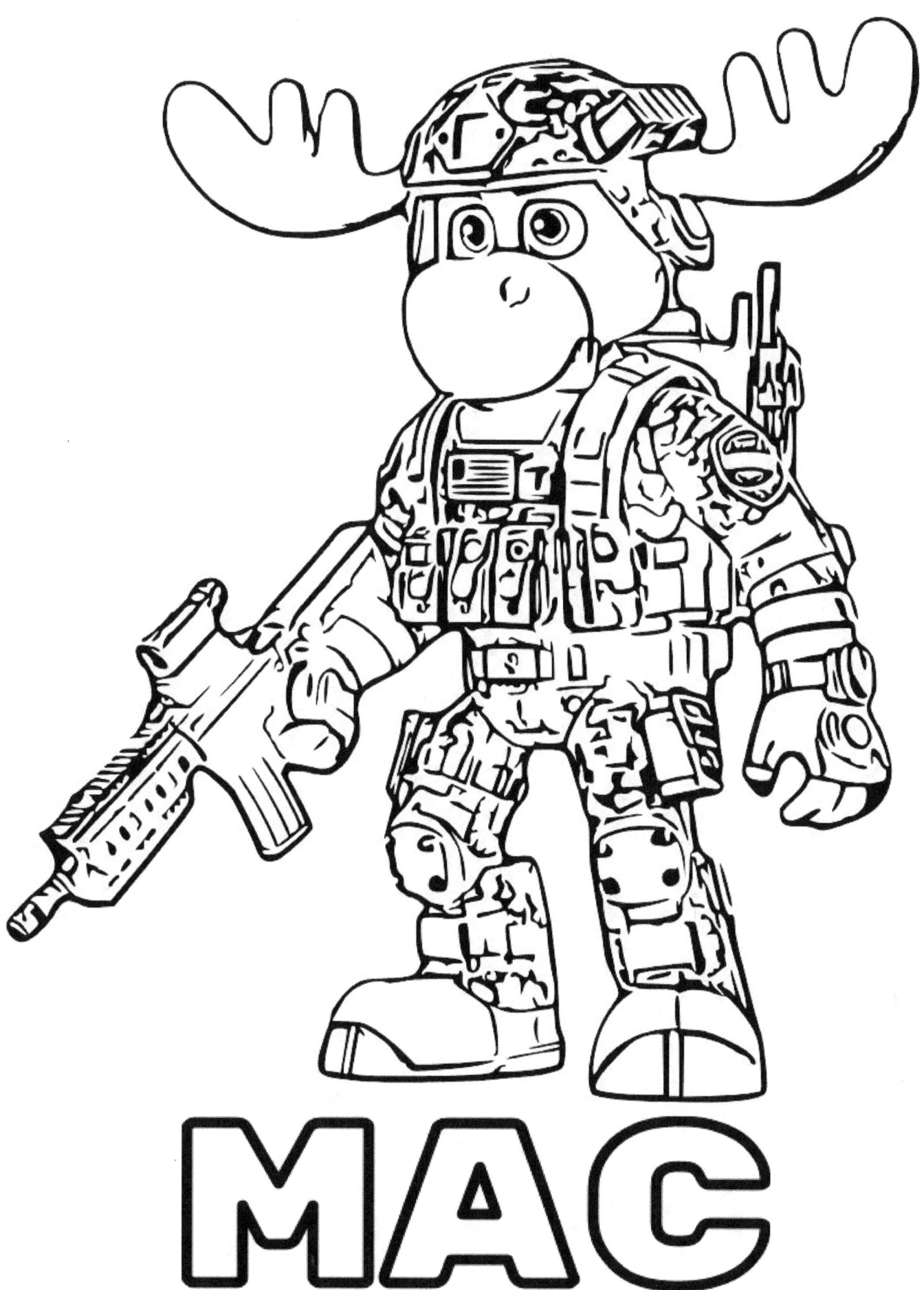

MAC

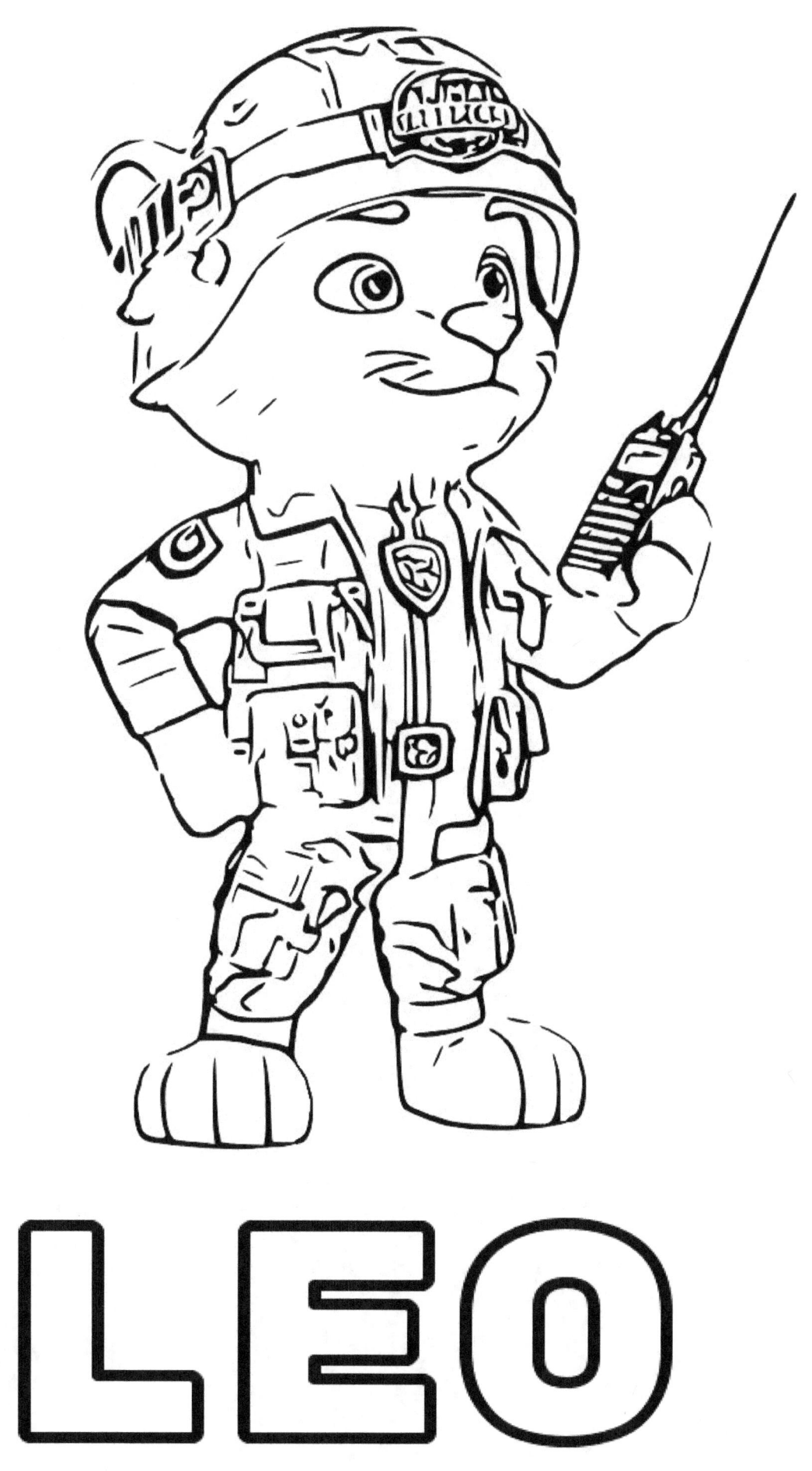

LEO

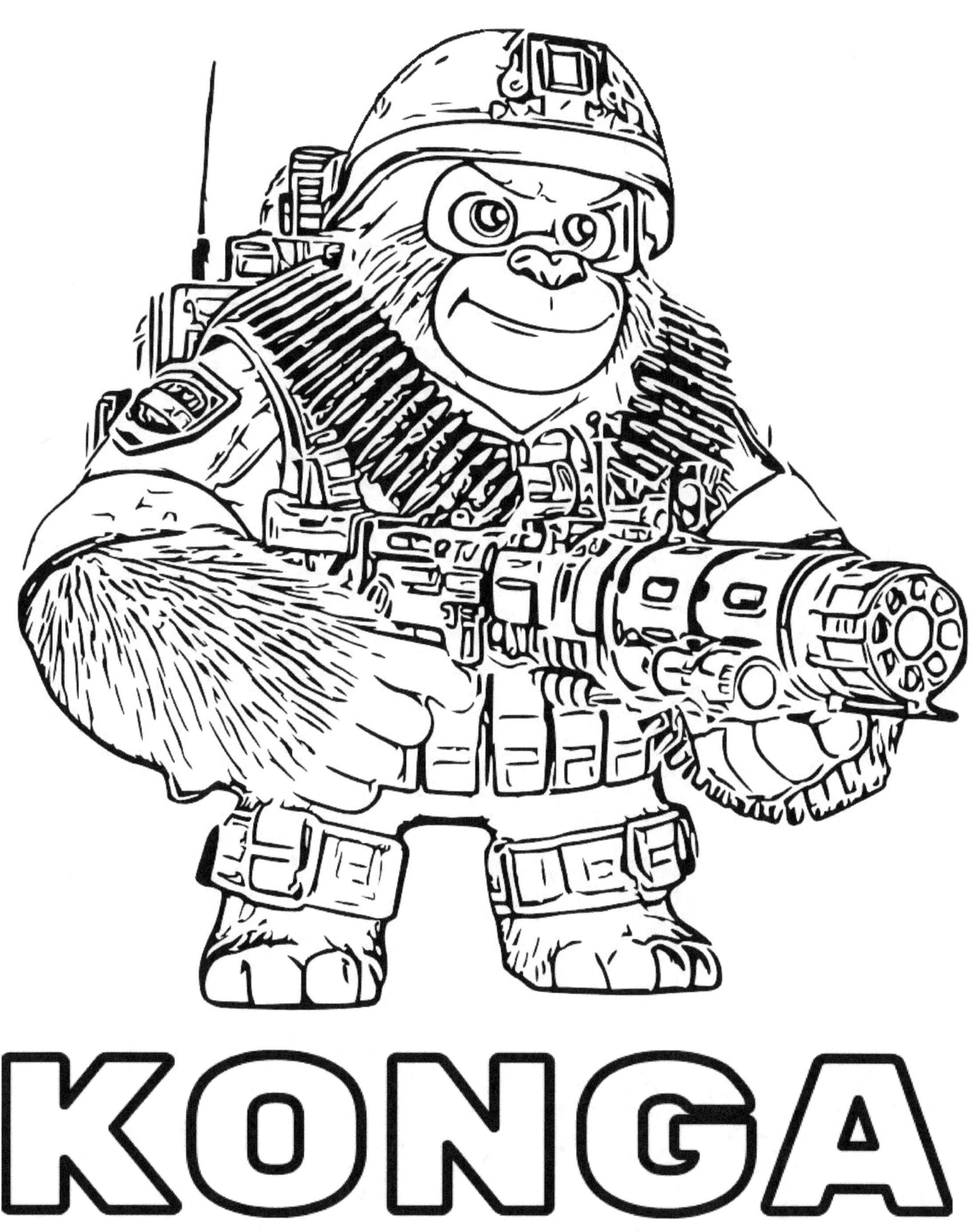

KONGA

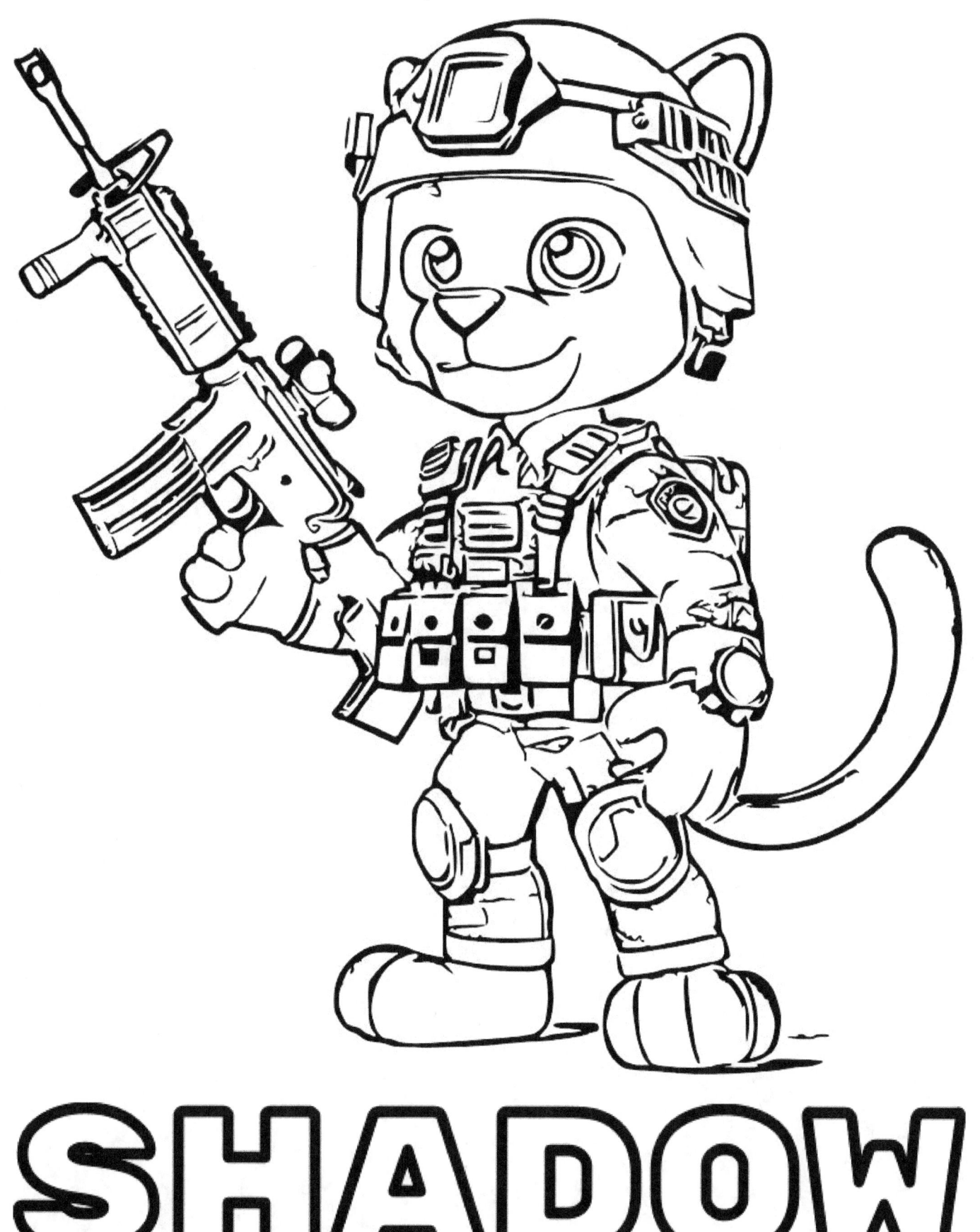

SHADOW

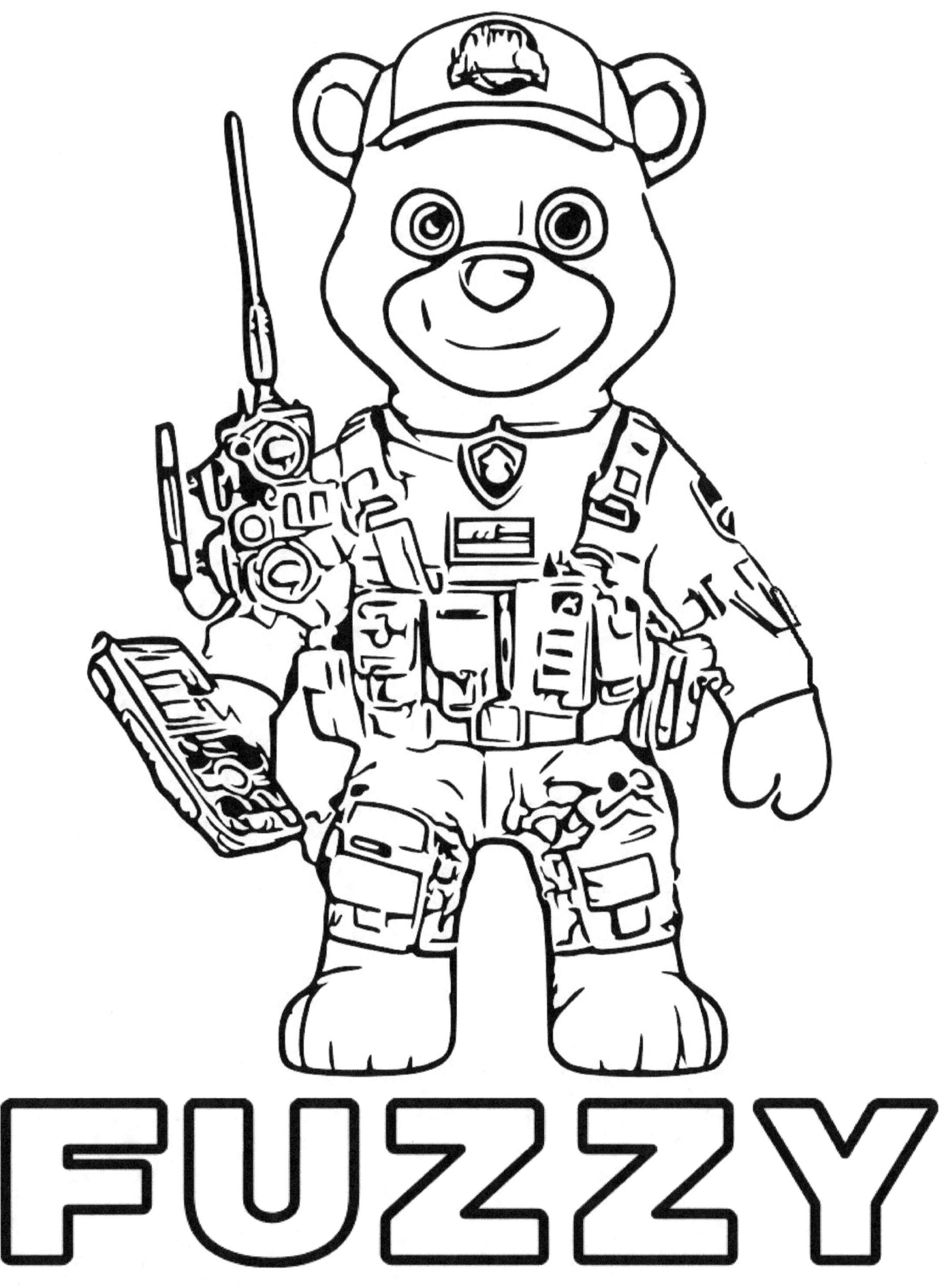

FUZZY

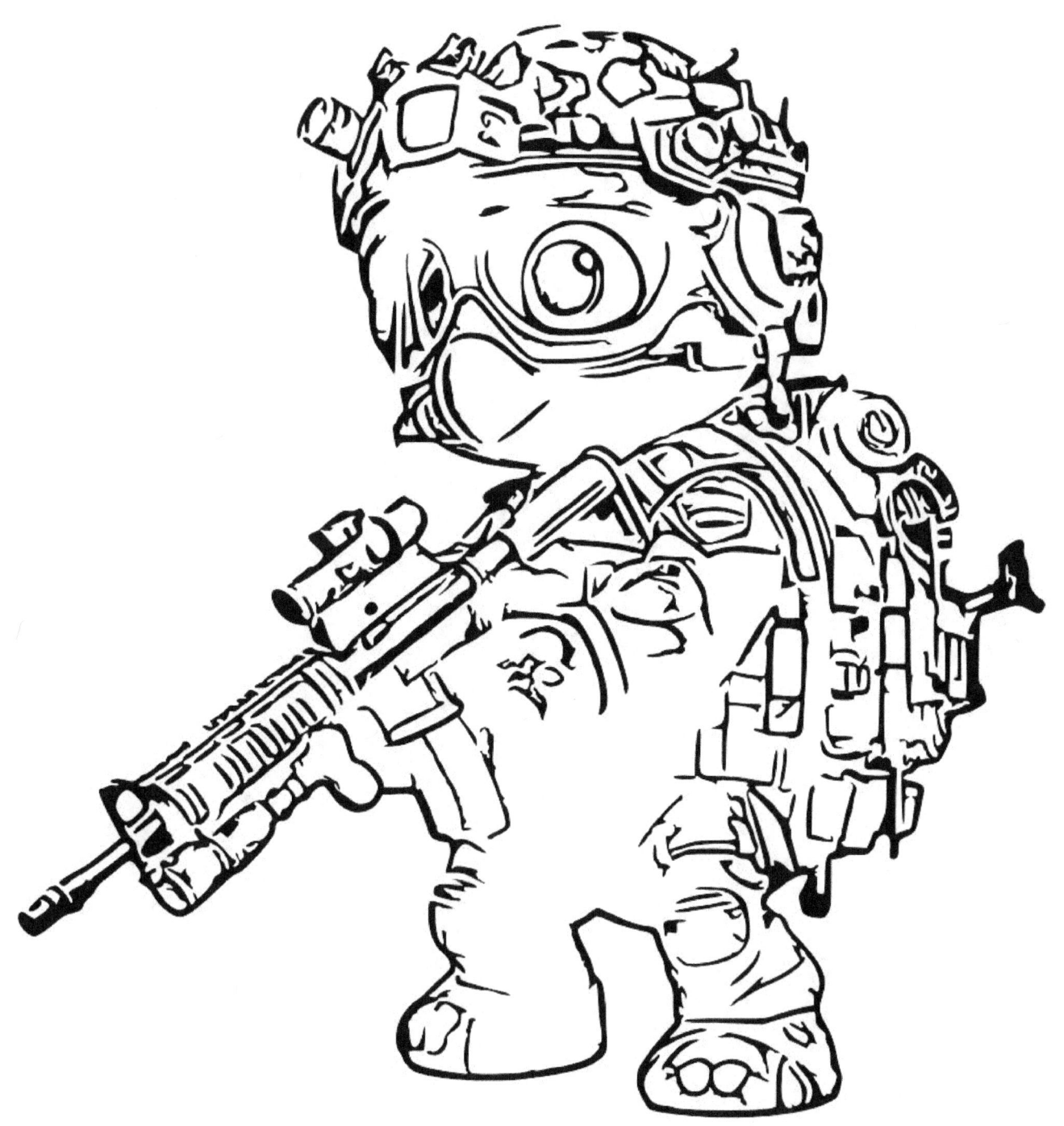

SHELLSHOCK

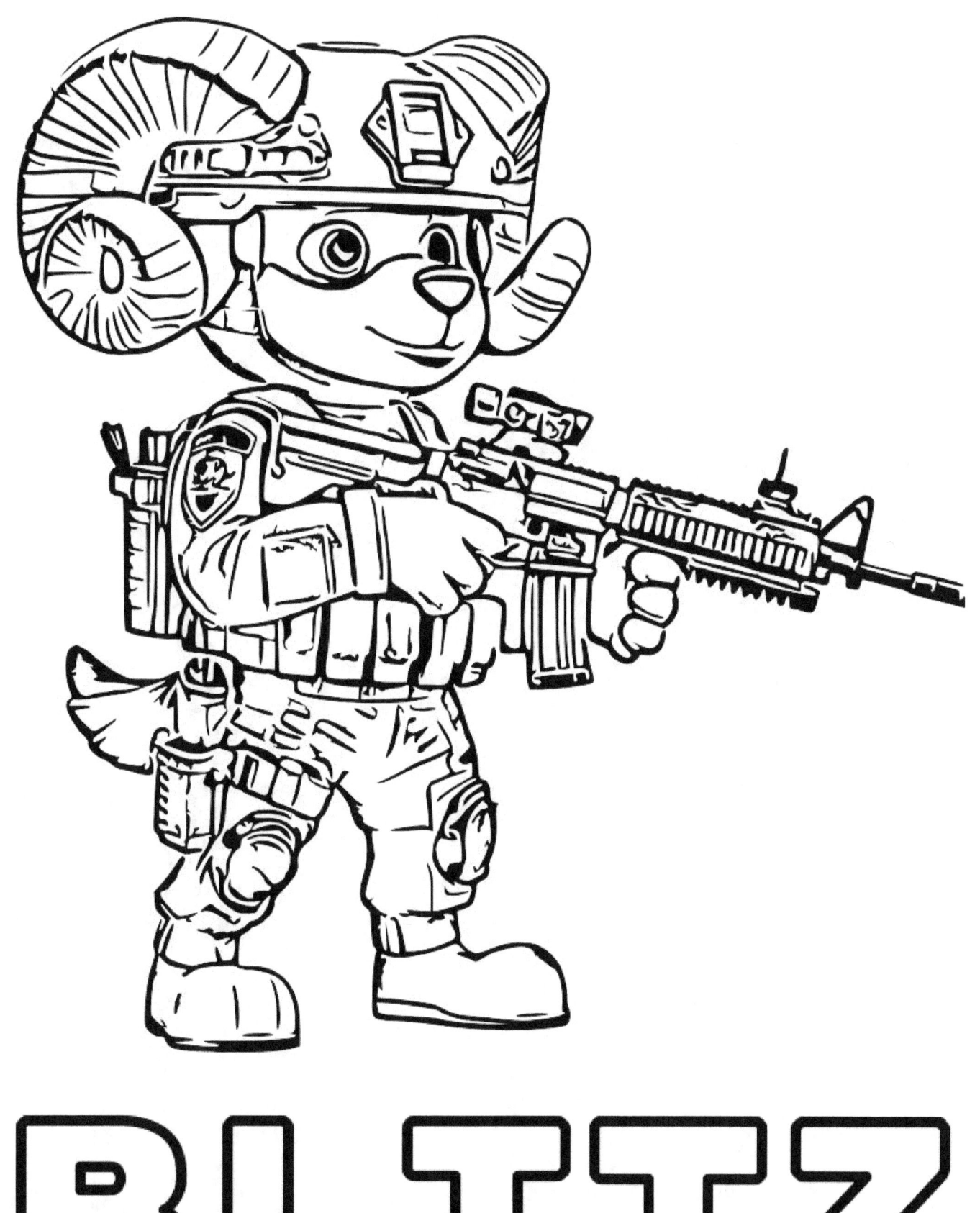

BLITZ

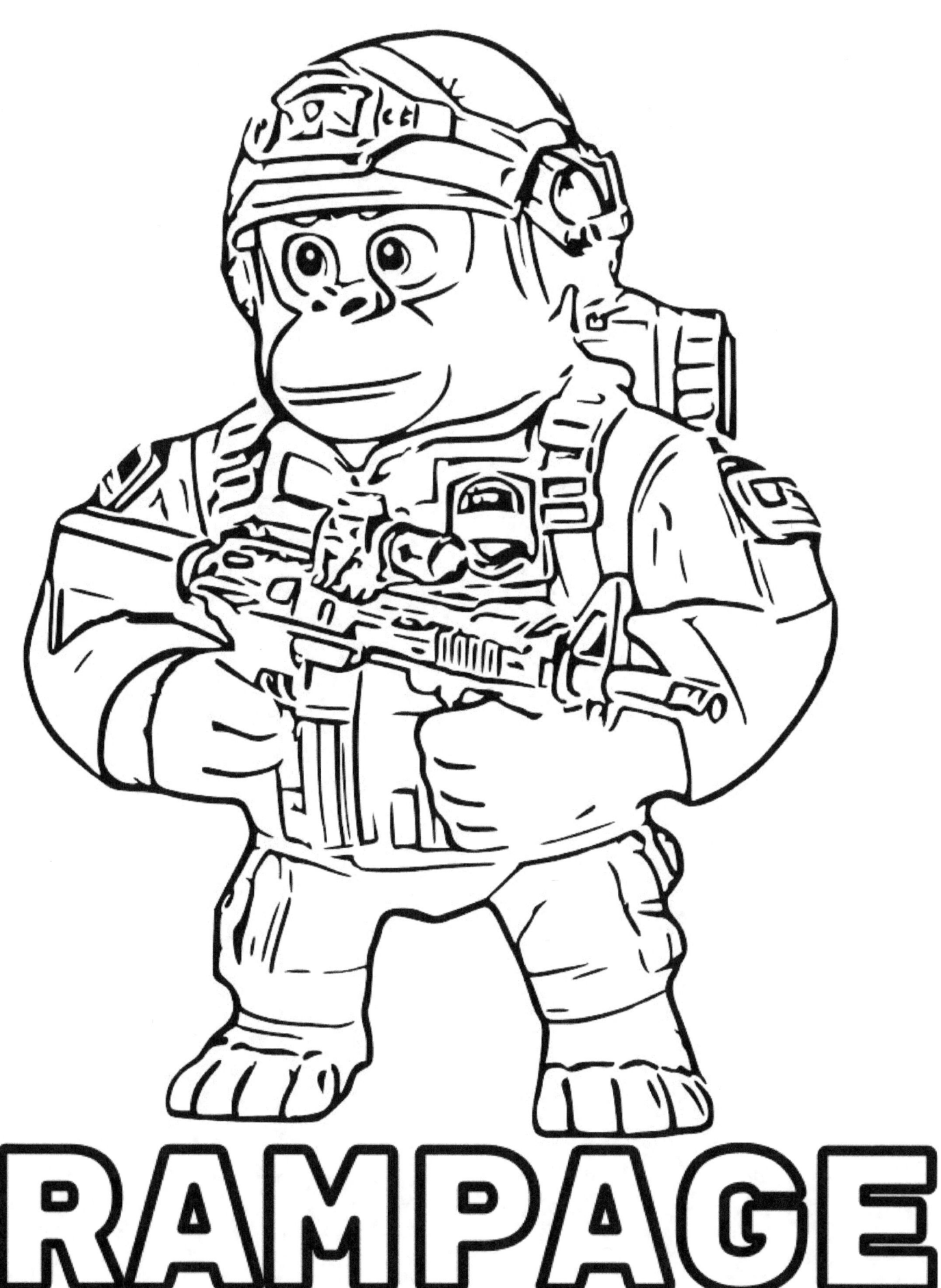

RAMPAGE

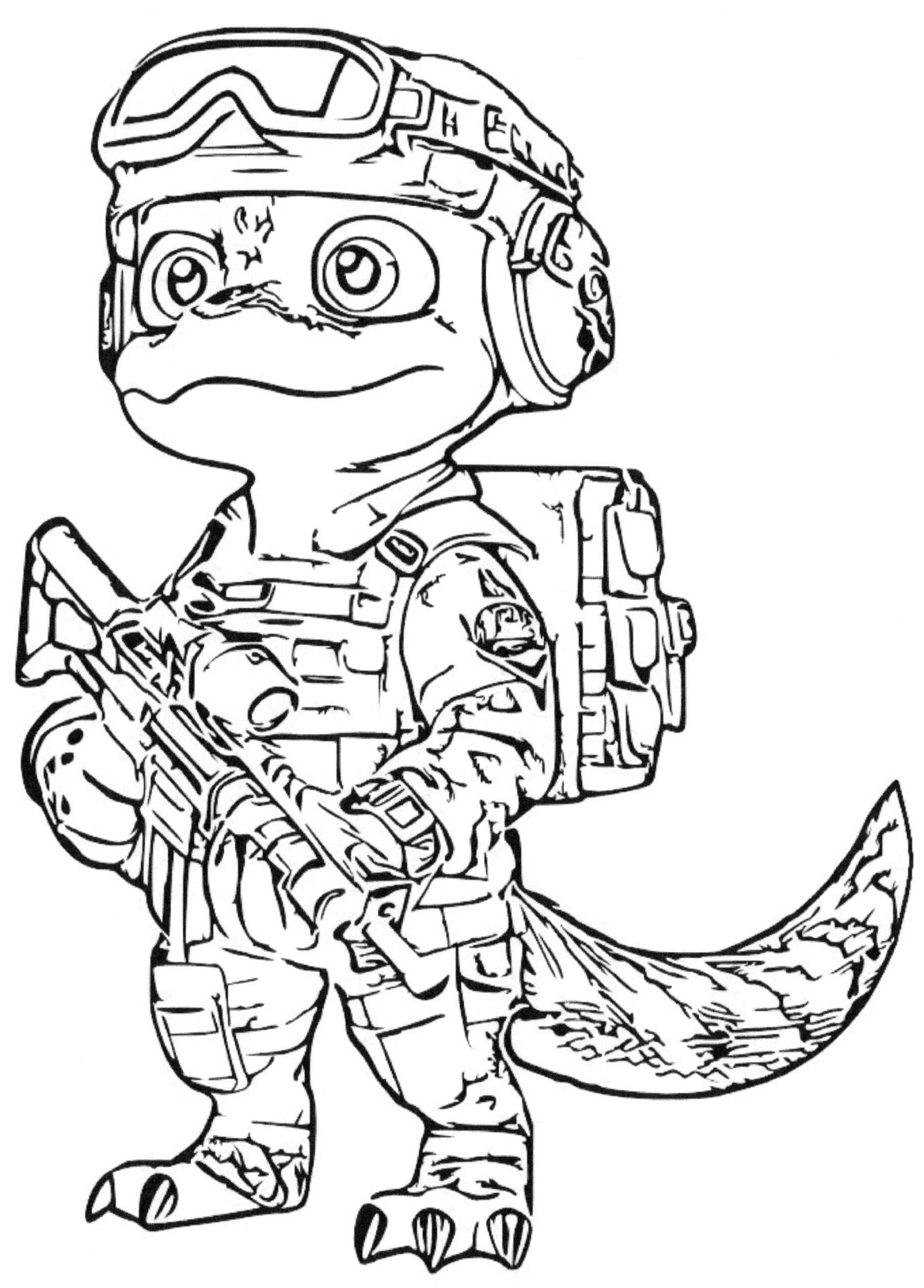

ROUGHSKIN

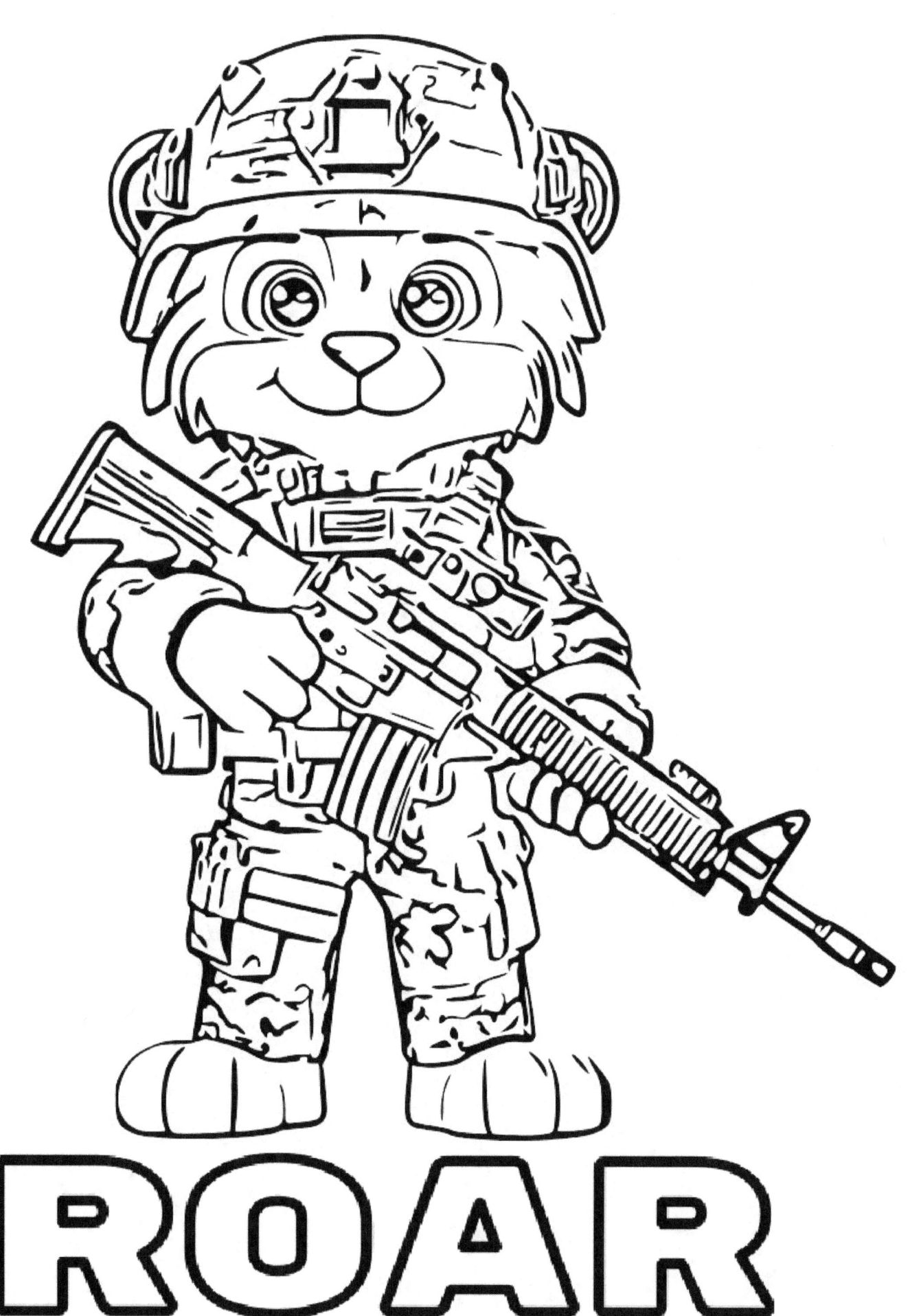

ROAR

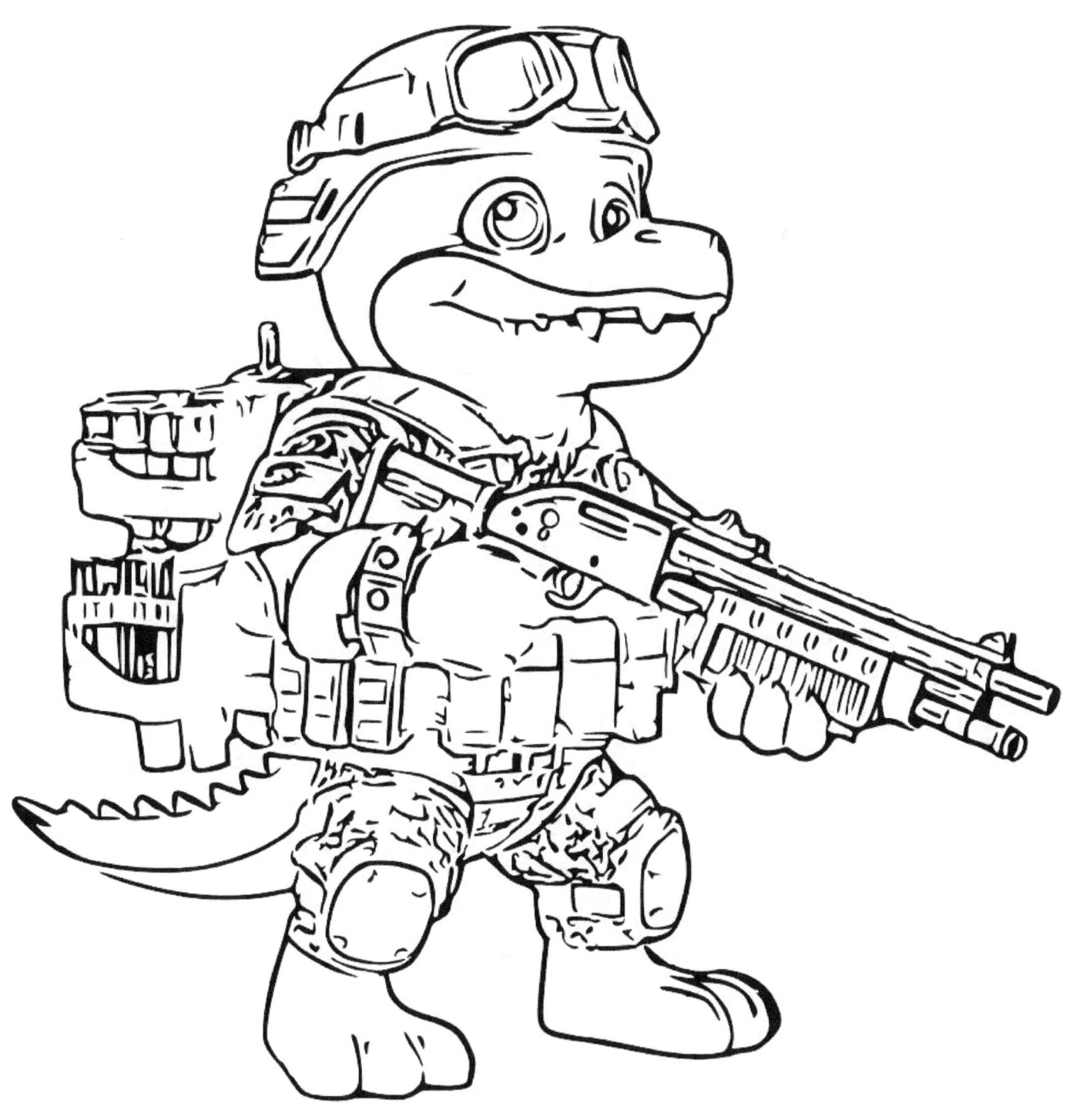

CRUNCH

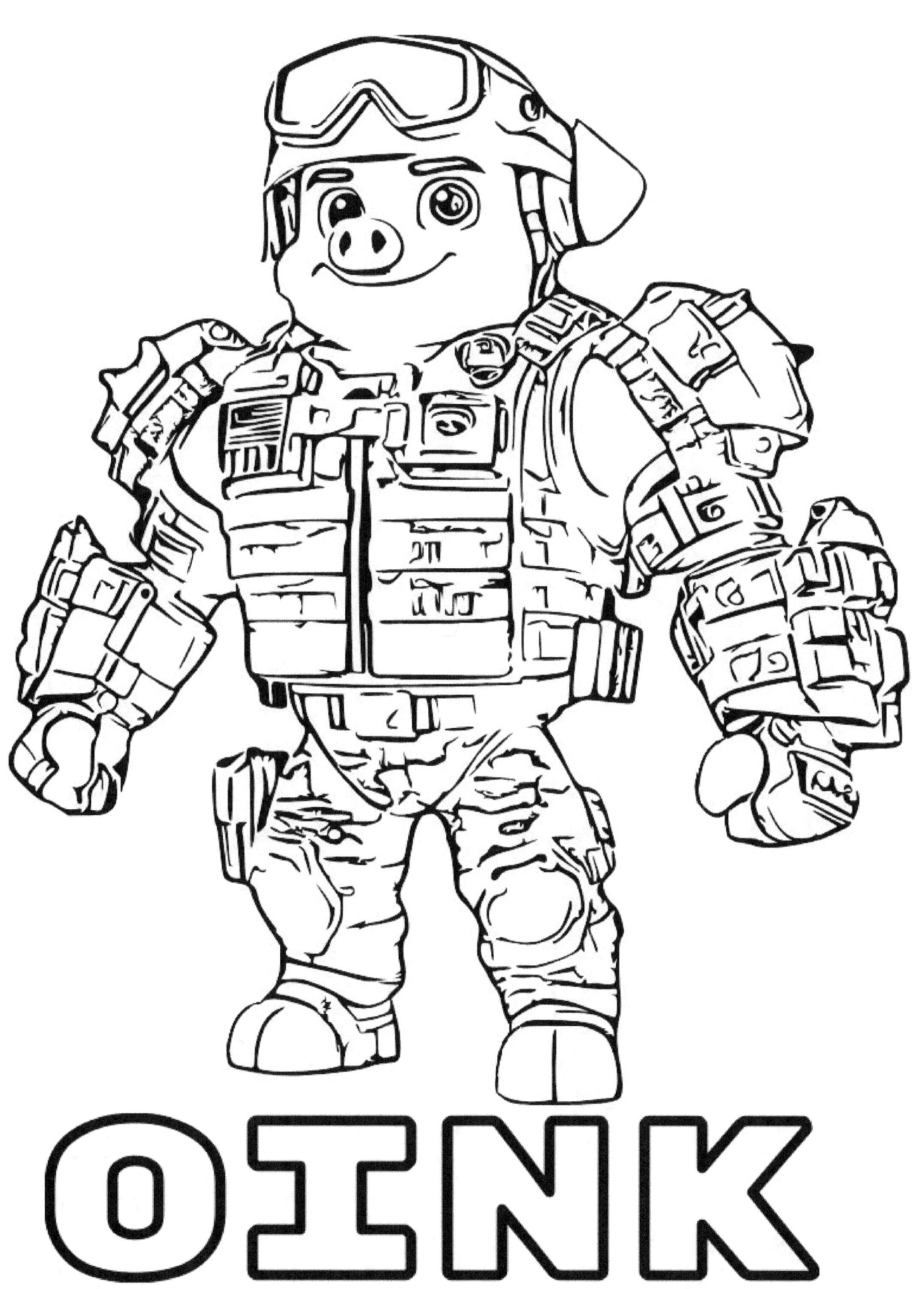

OINK

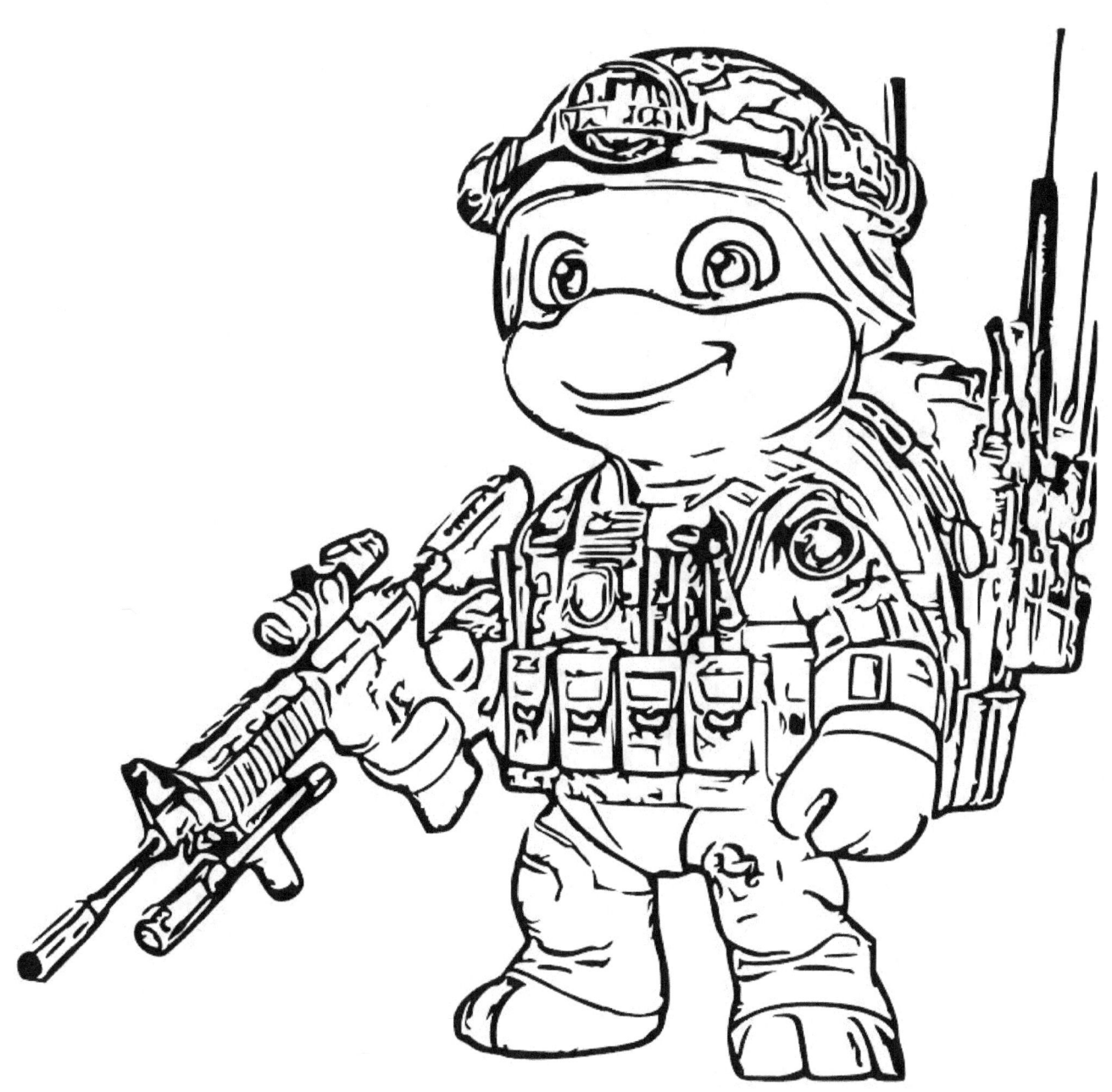

SNAPPER

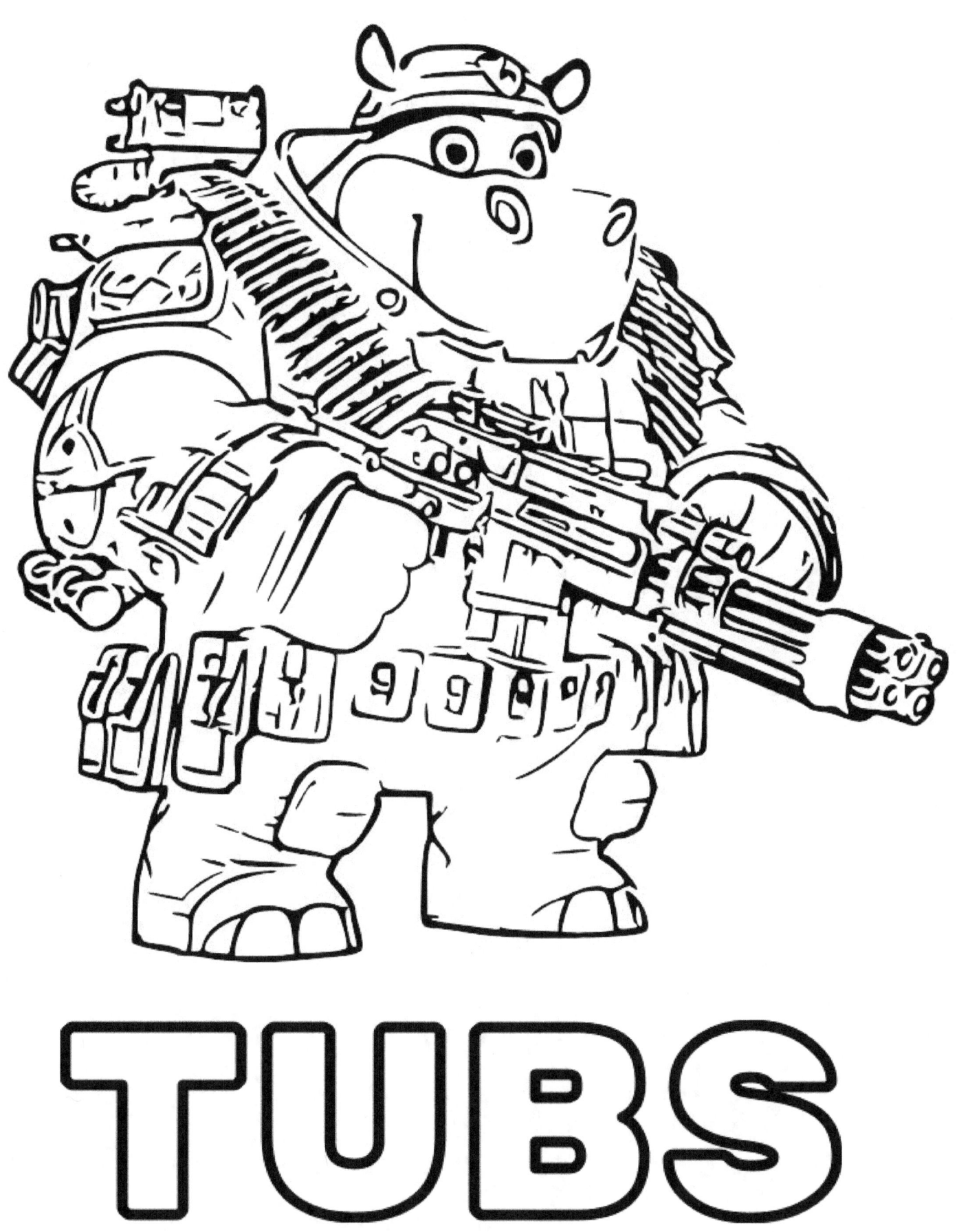

TUBS

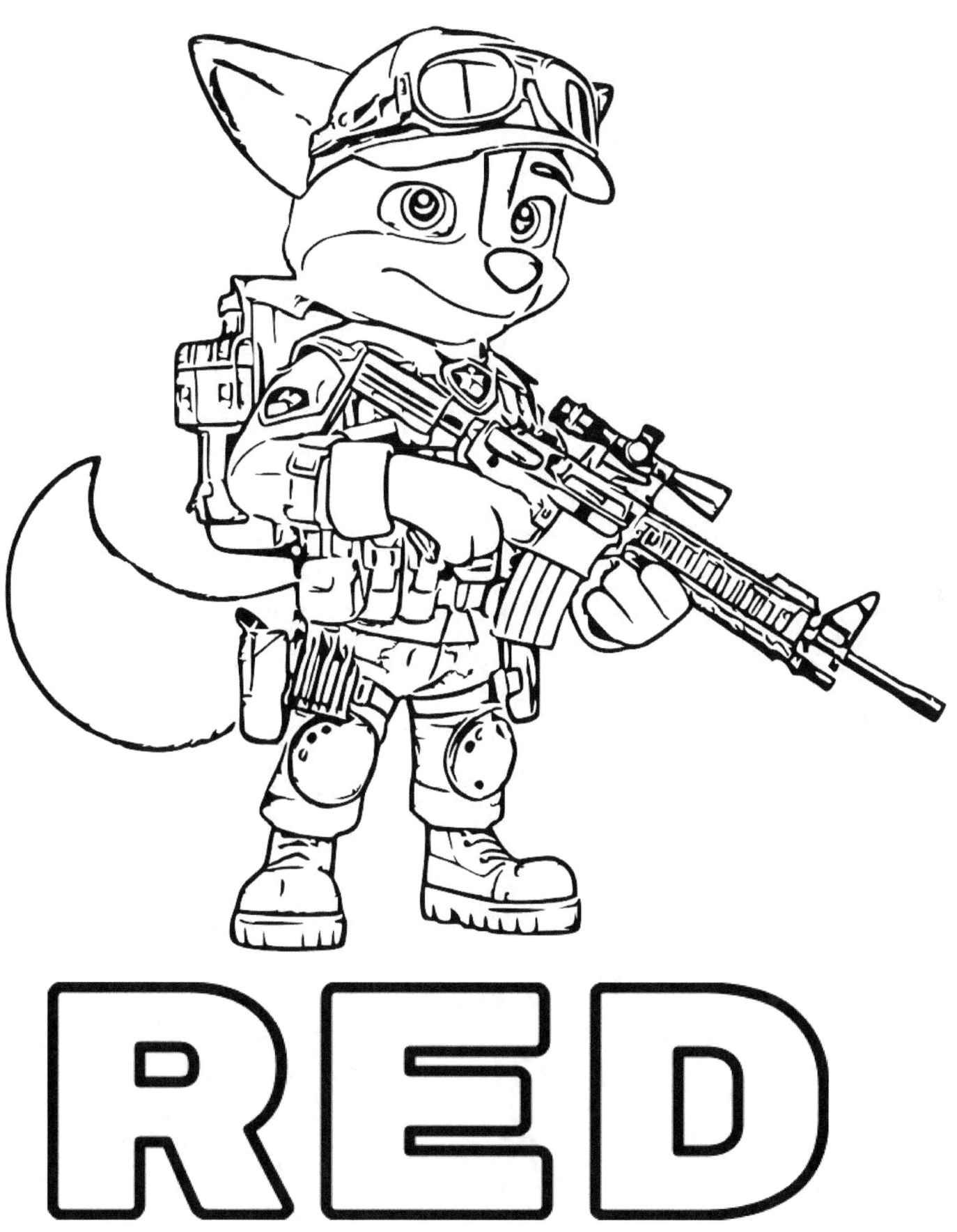

RED

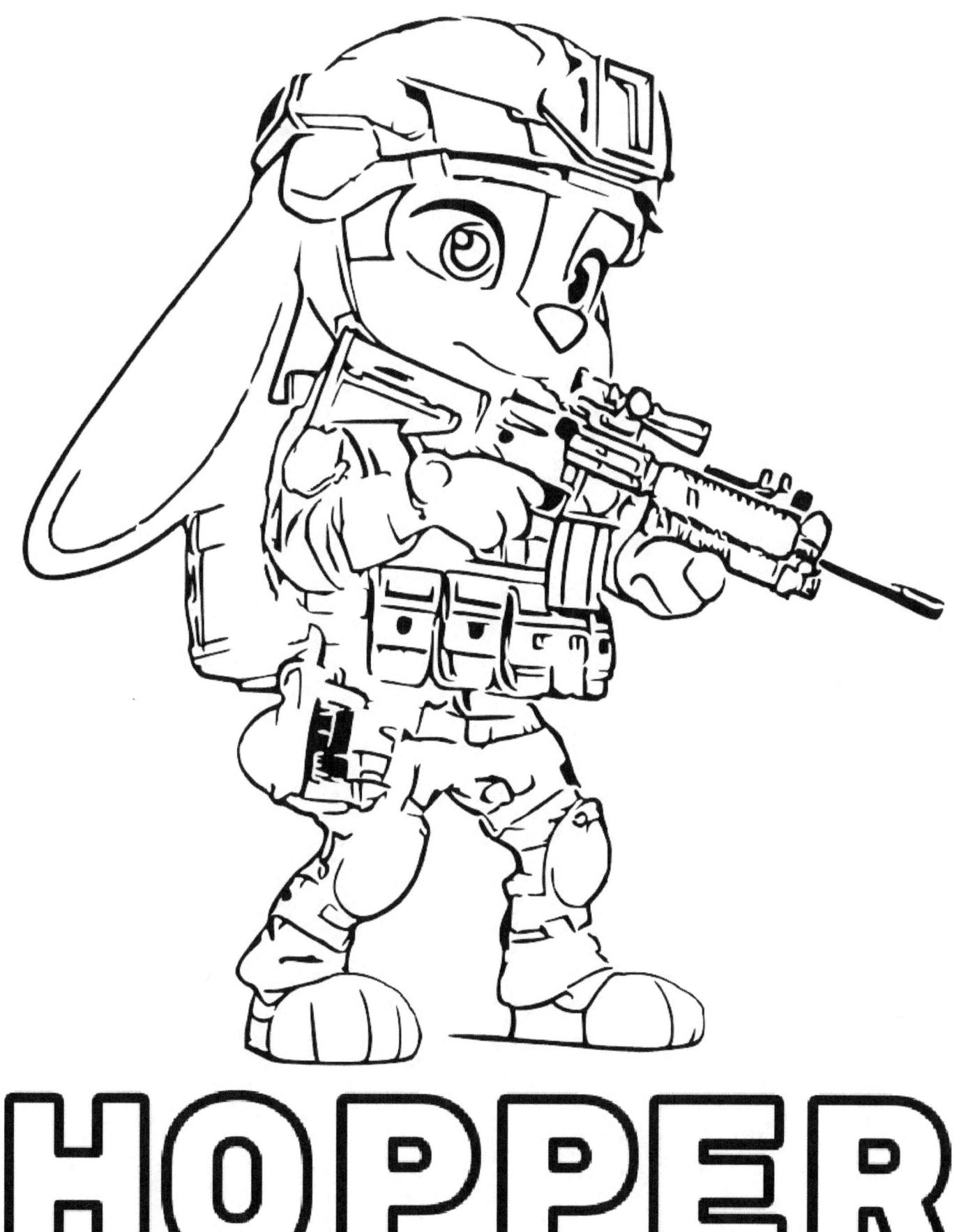

HOPPER

www.ingramcontent.com/pod-product-compliance
Lightning Source LLC
Chambersburg PA
CBHW060007230526
45472CB00008B/1984